About Starters

Starters books are written and designed with young readers in mind. They are vocabulary controlled and the contents have been carefully checked by a critic reader and teacher panel.

Each book contains questions for teacher-directed learning, bright and simple illustrations, interesting and informative text, picture glossary and a table of facts.

ISBN   0-88874-310-6

Edited by: GLC Editorial Department
Illustrations: Sigrid Schmitt
Critic Reader: Mrs. Margaret Knechtel, Reading Consultant, Etobicoke Board of Education
Teacher Panel: Miss Grace Davis, Grade 2 Teacher, Etobicoke Board of Education
Miss Maribel Hanson, Grade 2 Teacher, Etobicoke Board of Education

Printed by: Ashton-Potter Limited
Film Preparation: Graphic Litho-plate Inc.
Bound by: The Hunter Rose Company Ltd.

Printed and Bound in Canada

Uniquely Canadian Materials from GLC Publishers Limited
115 Nugget Avenue
Agincourt, Ontario

British Columbia is one of Canada's four
western provinces.
British Columbia is a beautiful province.
It has many mountains, lakes and waterfalls.

1

Victoria is the capital city of British Columbia.
It is on Vancouver Island.
Flowers bloom all year round in Victoria.

2

This is an undersea aquarium in Victoria.
You can watch sea creatures through a glass wall.

3

Vancouver is a busy seaport on the mainland.

Stanley Park is a beautiful park in Vancouver.
People have picnics or visit the zoo or aquarium.

There are many mountains in British Columbia.
There are three mountain ranges.

6

Some of the tallest trees in the world
grow in British Columbia.
They are called Douglas fir trees.
Douglas fir trees are often over six hundred
years old.

There are many islands off the coast
of British Columbia.
of British Columbia.
Vancouver Island is the biggest.

Here is Butchart Gardens.
Butchart Gardens was once a rock quarry
on Vancouver Island.
Now it is a beautiful garden.

There is good farmland in British Columbia.

apples

peaches

grapes

cherries

pears

strawberries

blueberries

raspberries

Many farmers in the Okanagan Valley grow fruit.

These fishermen are fishing for salmon, herring, or halibut.

12

Fishermen catch different kinds of salmon.
Some are sent to canneries.
Salmon is sold fresh or frozen.

This lumberjack is cutting down trees
with a chain saw.
Most trees go to a sawmill to be made into lumber.

14

Sometimes lumberjacks have contests.
Who can stay on a rolling log the longest?
Who can throw an ax and hit the target?
Who can saw a log the fastest?

There is gold in the mountains of
British Columbia.
Many miners "panned" for gold.

lumber

canned fish

paper

ships

dairy products

furniture

meat

big trucks

sugar

fruit products

These things are made in factories
in British Columbia.

People come to British Columbia
for their holidays.

18

Whistler Mountain is one of Canada's best
ski ranges.
One of the ski runs is over eleven kilometres long.

mountain goats

elk

cougar

black bear

moose

grizzly bear

These animals are found in the mountains and forests of British Columbia.

20

sea lions

porpoises

shrimps

crabs

killer whales

seals

These creatures are found in the ocean near
British Columbia.

Some people say they have seen a mysterious
monster in Okanagan Lake.
They have named the monster "Ogopogo."

Sasquatch

Another mysterious monster is said to live
in the forests of British Columbia.

Many different Indian tribes live
in British Columbia.
They fish for salmon.
They carved totem poles long ago.

White people came to trade with the Indians
for furs.
Railroad builders also came.
Many miners looked for gold.

PICTURE GLOSSARY

island
(page 2)

Douglas fir tree
(page 7)

aquarium
(page 3)

rock quarry
(page 9)

fishermen
(page 12)